Dear Parents,

Congratulations for choosing a fun and entertaining way to help your child learn to interact with others in pleasing, socially acceptable ways!

Children have the ability to be good, and they are often eager to please. However, they often don't understand their own egocentric or self-centered behavior. This self-centeredness often leads to misbehavior, and the misbehavior often leads to negative responses from others. All too soon, your child can be caught in a destructive cycle of negative action and reaction.

The purpose of the HELP ME BE GOOD books is to help your child break the cycle of negative action and reaction. Your child will learn how to replace misbehavior with acceptable behavior. Each HELP ME BE GOOD book is designed to do the following in an enjoyable way:

1. Define a misbehavior
2. Explain the cause of the misbehavior
3. Discuss the negative effects of the misbehavior
4. Offer suggestions for replacing the misbehavior with acceptable behavior

While it is effective to read the individual HELP ME BE GOOD books when a need arises, the series was designed to follow the normal development of young children. Consequently, presenting the books to your child in the order in which they are listed on the back cover of this book also works well.

As you and your child read the HELP ME BE GOOD books, your child will develop good behavior that will help build positive self-esteem and healthy relationships. Reading the books will also help to create a more friendly, happy atmosphere in your home. Thank you for allowing me to be a part of this exciting endeavor!

Sincerely,

Joy Berry

Joy Berry

Copyright © 2008 by Joy Berry
All rights reserved. Published by Joy Berry Enterprises, Inc., 146 West 29th St., Suite 11RW, New York, NY 10001

No part of this publication may be reproduced in whole or in part, or stored in a retrieval system, or transmitted in any form or by any means, electronic, mechanical, photocopying, recording, or otherwise, without written permission of the author. For information regarding permission write to Joy Berry,

Joy Berry Enterprises, Inc.
146 West 29th St., Suite 11RW
New York, NY 10001

Cover Design & Art Direction: John Bellaud
Art Production: Geoff Glisson
All music remastered at Midtown Sound Studios NYC, 2008

Printed in Mexico

ISBN 978-1-60577-104-5

A Help Me Be Good Book About

Being Messy

Adrian Branch Library
PO Box 39
Adrian, MN 56110
31315001803548
J-MM Berry
Being messy
1 book & 1 cd, in case

Written By Joy Berry
Illustrated by Bartholomew

Copyright © 2008 by Joy Berry

This book is about Annie.

Reading about Annie can help you understand and deal with ***being messy.***

WHAT A MESS!
I'LL SAY!

You are being messy when you

- spill food on your clothes or
- drop food on the furniture or floor.

YOU'RE MAKING A MESS WITH YOUR FOOD.
HUH?
SPILLING FOOD ON YOUR PET IS BEING MESSY!

You are being messy when you

- walk into clean areas with dirty feet,
- touch furniture or walls with dirty hands, or
- sit on furniture while wearing dirty clothes.

YOU'RE MAKING A **MESS** BY GETTING DIRT ALL OVER EVERYTHING !
YOU SHOULD SEE THE FLOOR.

You are being messy when you do not put your trash and garbage in appropriate containers.

YOU'RE MAKING A MESS!
PLINK

You are being messy when you

- do not put things away after you use them,
- do not put things where they belong, or
- do not put things away neatly.

IT'S HARD TO FIND THINGS WHEN YOU'RE MESSY.
GULP!

You are being messy when you are careless with things such as crayons, paints, pens, clay, or glue. You are being messy when you get things on your clothes or your surroundings.

CAN YOU GUESS WHAT I'M MAKING?
IT LOOKS LIKE YOU'RE MAKING A MESS.
YEAH, THAT WOULD HAVE BEEN MY GUESS.
ALL ABOUT EASTER

A mess can be *displeasing*.

Most people enjoy cleanliness, order, and beauty. A mess is not clean. It is not orderly. It is not beautiful. A mess does not make people happy. It usually makes them unhappy.

I DON'T
LIKE THE MESS
I MADE.
WE DON'T LIKE
IT EITHER!
ME
NEITHER!

A mess can be *frustrating*. People might become upset if they cannot find what they are looking for because

- it is hidden by clutter or
- it is not where it belongs.

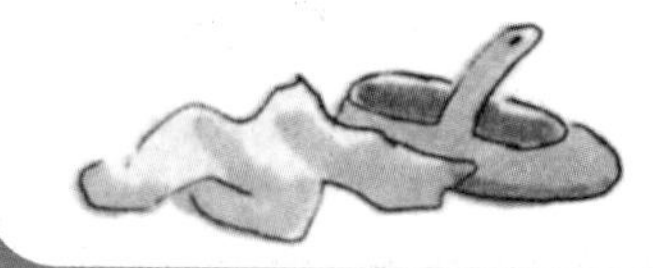

I **CAN'T** FIND MY OTHER SHOE!
NO ONE COULD FIND ANYTHING IN THIS MESS!
YOU SHOULD HAVE PUT YOUR SHOES IN THE CLOSET WHERE THEY BELONG!
IT'S SO CROWDED IN HERE I HAVE TO GO OUTSIDE TO CHANGE.

A mess can be *destructive.*

- Your clothes and surroundings can be ruined by messy stains.
- Things that are left out can be damaged accidentally.
- Things that are not put away carefully can be ruined.

UH-OH!
YOU SPILLED PAINT ON THE TABLECLOTH!
YOU DIDN'T PUT MY PAINTS AWAY AND NOW THEY'RE ALL DRIED OUT!
YOU RUINED THIS PAPER BY STUFFING IT IN THE DRAWER.
NOT TO MENTION RUINING MY FUR!

A mess can be *dangerous.*

- People can slip and possibly fall because of messy spills.
- People can trip over things that are out of place.

DID YOU REMEMBER TO PICK UP YOUR TOYS ?
OH NO! LAST WEEK HE SLIPPED ON A BANANA PEEL I DROPPED.
ZING

Messes can be

- displeasing,
- frustrating,
- destructive, and
- dangerous.

This is why you should not be messy.

An accident can cause a mess. You can avoid accidental messes by *being careful*.

IT WAS AN ACCIDENT.
I UNDERSTAND, BUT NEXT TIME YOU NEED TO BE MORE CAREFUL.
WHEW!

There are things you can do to avoid messes.

To prevent a mess:

- Cover your clothes before you do something that might be messy. (Use a napkin, apron, or smock.)
- Protect the area where you are working by covering it with newspapers, an old sheet, or a tablecloth.

THANK YOU FOR PUTTING NEWSPAPER UNDER YOUR EASEL, ANNIE.
OOPS! I'M SURE GLAD THERE WAS PAPER THERE.

To prevent a mess:

- Keep yourself and your clothes as clean as possible.
- Wash your hands before you touch clean things.
- Get the dirt, mud, or sand off your feet before you walk into a clean area.

THANK YOU FOR CLEANING THE MUD OFF YOUR SHOES BEFORE YOU COME INTO THE HOUSE.
WIPE WIPE

To prevent a mess:

- Do not litter. Put trash in a trash container. Put garbage in a garbage disposal or container.
- Put things away when you are finished using them. Put things away neatly where they belong.

YOU'RE DOING A GREAT JOB!
I'LL SAY!

You and the people around you will be happier if you avoid being messy.

NO MORE MESS!

Being Messy Song Lyrics

Music & Lyrics by Joy Berry & Craig K. Miller

You're Being Messy

You've thrown things on the floor.
It's hard to open up your door.
You've thrown trash all around.
It's hard for you to see the ground.

You're being messy,
Ma-ma-ma messy.
You're being messy,
Ma-ma-ma messy.

You are playing in the dirt.
There are stains on your pants and shirt.
When you walk through the door,
You leave tracks on the floor.

You're being messy,
Ma-ma-ma messy.
You're being messy,
Ma-ma-ma messy.

It's not hard to be neat.
Hang up your clothes, dust off your feet.
When you paint, cover up.
Throw out your trash, pick things up.

And don't be messy,
Ma-ma-ma messy.
Don't you be messy,
Ma-ma-ma messy.

And don't be messy,
Ma-ma-ma messy.
Don't you be messy,
Ma-ma-ma messy.

Messy Jessy

I'm going to tell you a story
About a girl I used to know.
Who always left a trail of garbage
Everywhere she'd go.

When anybody saw her coming
They'd run the other way,
And way off in the distance
You could hear them say:

Run for cover right away,
Hide your paints and glue and clay.
Once you let her in your door,
She'll make your house a mess for sure.

They called her Messy Jessy.

If you were eating at the table
With Jessy next to you,
You would have to wear a raincoat
Cuz by the time she's through,
Jessy spilled her food and drinks on
Everything in sight.
You'd have to keep your distance
Or you'd look a fright!

Run for cover don't look back
Hide your food and drink and snack.
Once you let her in your door
You'd have one big mess for sure!

They called her Messy Jessy.

Oh Jessy, ever so messy.
Finally it hit her, the clutter and litter.
How very depressing, enough of this messing!
I want to clean up now! Except, I don't know how.

Jessy started in to learning
To be a neater one.
She had to change a lot of habits
Before the job was done.

But now when people see her coming
They open up their door,
She never will be Messy Jessy any more.

Run for cover, not so fast!
Jessy has turned neat at last.
She's a joy to have around.
She's the cleanest one in town.

So goodbye Messy Jessy.